DISCOVERING YOUR
MISSIONAL
POTENTIAL

DISCOVERING YOUR
MISSIONAL
POTENTIAL

AN ENCOUNTER WITH EPHESIANS 4
AND HOW JESUS LIVES IT

Daryl L. Smith and Andrew B. Smith

MOVEMENTS

DISCOVERING YOUR MISSIONAL POTENTIAL
—an encounter with Ephesians 4 and how Jesus lives it

© 2019 by Daryl L. Smith and Andrew B. Smith
First published in 2019 by 100M. 100Movements.com.

MOVEMENTS

Design and layout: Carolyn B. Smith

ISBN: 978-0-9986393-7-6

ENDORSEMENTS

"Daryl expertly unpacks FiveFold Ministry in a way that is accessible and engaging. The real skill is that while it is engaging, it is in no way shallow. The guide is deep and thoughtful as well as being very accessible and applicable for many.
I am excited to see this resource in the hands, around the tables, and in the conversations of many leaders who can find their place and play their part as the Church. It is an opportunity for the body of Christ to mature in a new season and for individuals to release their mission potential. This book is good news. And will help people live out good news."

~ *Rich Robinson*, Catalyst and Coach/CatalyseChange.org

Daryl and Andrew continue to carry the ball forward in the practical application of Ephesians 4 to the church. This highly accessible resource is great for gatherings and congregations of any size.

~ Jessie Cruickshank, co-author of *Activating 5Q: A User's Guide*; 100Movements lead driver

"The revelation of Scripture from Paul, the wisdom of experience from Daryl, and the outside-the-box application from Andrew—that's what you get in this book. And more, you get the opportunity to join the journey where you live and work."

~ *Steve Harper*, retired professor and United Methodist clergyperson

"One of the most promising conversations that has potential for wholesale change in the church today is around the Ephesians 4 typology of ministry (APEST). Even though it has been a part of the essential revelation on the church since the New Testament, the truth is that useful resources on topic are rare indeed. Daryl and Andrew have gifted us with a great small group resource in this book. I am grateful."

~ *Alan Hirsch*, author of *5Q* and founder of the 5Q Collective

THE AUTHORS

Daryl L. Smith has devoted his life to helping equip people for their ministry—whatever form that takes. He has taught Christian leadership and discipleship at the seminary level and is the creator of several outside-the-church resources for Bible study and missional living.

Andrew B. Smith works to help the church (and everyone in it) recapture the missional purpose that we see God leading us in throughout the Bible. He served in church ministry for 15 years before stepping into the non-profit world, helping to bring transformation to those in need in Orlando, Florida.

SPECIAL THANKS

As our first project together, this was a delightful process—merging our group experience (Daryl) and biblical insights (Andrew) into one piece of art.

To the many who contributed to make this a better work, we are grateful.

Among them are...

- **Demetria Childs, Pamela DeDea, Michael Gonyo, Charles Hughes, Adam Lauman, Alissa Rothschild, Matthew Russell, Andryl Spikes, Meagan Stone,** and **Aaron Vickroy**, members of CD/CL/SF613—*Recruiting and Equpping Laity*, at Asbury Theological Seminary—Florida (Fall 2018) who field-tested most of this material and offered great suggestions and corrections.

- **Carolyn Smith** for her copy-editing and design work, offering much-needed feedback.

- **Rich** and **Anna Robinson**, who encouraged, reviewed, and gave corrective suggestions.

- **Jessie Cruickshank**, who has become a treasured colleague and resource person.

- And many unnamed others, who have contributed deeply to our lives along the way.

DISCOVERING YOUR MISSIONAL POTENTIAL
—an encounter with Ephesians 4 and how Jesus lives it

GETTING STARTED...

God is up to something big in our world... and WE'RE called to join as partners.

OUR GOAL for this set of Village Group sessions is to help us discover how God has gifted people to accomplish Jesus' mission of transforming, renewing, and restoring our world. He wants to do that through us—all of us—everyday normal people; not just those who work inside a church facility.

That means discovering how we're called to live in the ways God has gifted us, both as a *community* and *individually*, so the "movement" of God reflects all of the fullness of its potential to bring transformation!

But we're not trying to figure out how we can be better ushers, choir members, or any other church role (as important as those are), because this is so much bigger than just what happens inside a building!

The letter St. Paul wrote to the Jesus-followers in Ephesus sits as a pinnacle book to guide us in understanding Jesus' mission-plan for his followers—the church. And chapter 4 in that letter to the Ephesians gives specific guidance in the ways Jesus wants to carry out his mission on this planet, through us.

The first persons to receive this letter would have understood the FIVE key gifting areas Paul describes: *Apostle, Prophet, Evangelist, Shepherd, Teacher* (A.P.E.S.T.). It may be harder for us to get our minds around these ancient words because either we have no idea what they mean or we may carry a pile of bad memories about them. But these concepts lay a wide foundation for how the church's mission can be lived out—utilizing the fullness and diversity of how we're created.

Jesus lived out these five areas perfectly. Paul says that Jesus then gave these gifts to the church for fulfilling its function of helping Jesus-followers grow to maturity.

As disciples of Jesus, with his image planted in us, we too have an APEST Profile—all five gift areas. And we will discover that, unlike Jesus, we each reflect certain strengths or passions for some gift areas, while others are weaker. (We're not 20%, 20%, 20%, 20%, 20%.) However, those weaker areas will become the places where we (with the aid of God's Spirit) help one another grow as Jesus-followers (disciples)—being shaped more into the image of Jesus for the sake of others.

Remember, it's only together that we, as Jesus' body, express the fullness of these gift areas. So, there will be people sitting next to us who have insights we don't have. And hopefully we'll have some for them!

Our study focus starts in Ephesians 4, where Paul talks specifically about the unity and diversity that leads to maturity in Jesus-followers—the church. He describes how we're different, but all integral, and how Jesus handed off his earthly mission for us to accomplish (renewing and restoring the world). We are each called to identify and carry out our vocational part of that broader mission, living into our gifting areas or passions.

After the first **THREE** sessions we'll look at how Jesus lived out these five gifting areas (APEST) in his own ministry. Hopefully, as we examine his modeling, we'll better understand our role in his missional call for us.

While our specific gift areas will help the church, they are not meant just to benefit those in the church community. In fact, much of how we live out these gift passions should happen in the "marketplace"—everyday moments and everyday locations—at work, with our neighbors, or at play. This is where our part in Jesus' mission becomes transformational to the world around us.

However, you may be joining this group as someone who's not part of any faith community. Or you may have big questions about the whole "God-thing." That's great.

We hope that, as you explore, you'll discover more of how you've been *wired* and how you may already be living out your own unique gifting.

CLARIFYING A FEW TERMS

■ A.P.E.S.T. further defined

To further translate Paul's "gifting" terms, check out these expanded definitions. Soon you will want to complete *The A.P.E.S.T. Personal Vocational Assessment* (www.5Qcentral.com) to find out which of the gift areas may be your strongest, and which of the five you may need to grow in.

(A) Apostle—visionary, risk-taker, connects the pieces, strategist, bridge builder to new contexts.

(P) Prophet—truth-teller, justice-minded, advocate, reformer, speaker for God.

(E) Evangelist—promoter, enthusiastic, recruiter, finds creative ways to share the message, motivator.

(S) Shepherd—care-giver, community builder, peacemaker, protector, defender.

(T) Teacher—shares wisdom and insight, equips others, passes along the heritage

That should get you started dreaming. And you may already recognize yourself in one or more of these areas.

Just remember, these broad terms lay a foundation for how the church (all Jesus-followers) is to function and what's needed for the mission to succeed. If you've come across some of Paul's other lists of *gifts*, you will begin to see that they are suggestions of how these larger categories play out, specifically.

For example, on the *Assessment*, your strongest gift area may be *Shepherd*, and you cannot imagine yourself as the pastor of a church. However, if you're a person who is concerned about caring for others (like visiting shut-ins, gathering people together, cooking meals, helping where needed, etc.) that could be the specific way that you're living out your larger *Shepherd* gift area.

In addition it's vital to remember that Paul's encouragement to develop what he calls the "Fruit of the Spirit" in Galatians 5:22–23 (love, joy, peace patience, kindness, goodness, faithfulness, gentleness, self-control),

becomes the personal soil out of which we grow in our missional vocation...
as God's Spirit transforms us from the inside out.

So, like a sports team, we're not all defenders, or attackers, or midfielders.
But we play our diverse parts to bring about a unified win. In a similar way,
a company has various employees who fill diverse roles—all working for the
same company.

What is 5Q?

At some point you'll start seeing the term *5Q*. Don't let that throw you.
Just as the term IQ is used to describe a person's *Intelligence Potential, 5Q*
was coined as a term to describe five-fold *Missional Potential* so we can ask
how effectively all five APEST gifting areas are lived out in a community of
Jesus-followers.

Thus, *5Q Central* is a network of people who've committed themselves to
helping Jesus-followers grow in living as disciples of Jesus—to help us
effectively carry out Jesus' mission—using our APEST vocations to fulfill
Jesus' call to make disciples.

Mission or Vocation?

You will note that the terms *calling, mission, ministry,* and *vocation* are often
used interchangeably, depending on the context. They all refer to God's
desire for us to participate, and fulfill our part in making disciples of Jesus
and doing God's Kingdom work on Earth.

The Village Group Model

You may be familiar with some form of Bible study or small group. A *Village
Group* goes well beyond a typical small group. Here's a brief explanation of
why *Village Group* describes what should happen whenever a group of 6–12
people gather to study the Bible, life, and mission.

- This group is designed around three stories: God's story (the Bible), Your Story, and My Story. Every time we meet we each get to tell part of our stories and see how they connect to God's story. This is called *Relational Bible Study.*

- Researchers have shown that:

  1. When we learn through story, rather than just memorizing facts, our entire brains come alive; we naturally remember and apply the learning to future situations in our lives.[1]

  2. In order for us to actually learn *anything* about relating to God or one another, we must wrestle with those concepts in a small group setting—practicing them in a safe place.[2]

  3. In addition, these group sessions are designed to connect to each of our learning preferences. Some of us need to start by knowing **WHY** we need to learn something. Others of us just want to know the content—**WHAT**. Still others of us are primarily concerned with **HOW** to use what we're learning. Then, some of us dream about **WHAT ELSE** we could do with what we learn.[3]

- Finally, think of this group as a Village, a place where:

  ... Everyone belongs,

  ... People are safe to be themselves,

  ... Everyone is being equipped for ministry/service,

  ... Everyone is cared for,

  ... There is a common purpose or mission, AND

  ... You can always come home.

Notes

1. Jessica Cruickshank—a demonstrated disciple-maker and facilitator of spiritual transformation. Jesse is an ordained Foursquare minister and a nationally recognized leader in the fields of experiential eduation and educational neuroscience. She holds a master's degree from Harvard University in Mind, Brain and Education. Jesse is passionate about creating organic systems that facilitate holistic human and organizational development.

2. Lev Vygotsky—a Russian psychologist (1896—1934) discovered that social values are best learned when experimented with (tried out) in social settings.

3. See Bernice McCarthy at About Learning, Inc., Wauconda, IL. Check out her *The Learning Cycle, The 21st-Century and Millennial Learners* (About Learning, 2012). ISBN: 978-1929040049. Available at www.AboutLearning.com or www.Amazon.com.

SESSION 1: LIVING IN UNITY

THE CONTEXT

We're picking up with Paul in the middle of his letter to the Jesus-followers in the ancient Roman city of Ephesus. If we read the letter from the beginning, we will see that Paul's desire is to paint a clear picture of the massive scope of God's purpose (through Jesus) to renew and restore everything (including all of "heaven and earth"), and to help the Ephesians see their integral role in that plan.

Here in chapter 4, we can immediately see Paul's personal passion and urgency for this mission and his willingness to do whatever that mission might require. He's writing from a Roman prison (a fact he has already reminded them of several times). While imprisonment would have been a disgrace in Roman culture, and even possibly made some question his leadership credentials, he's clear on his willingness to accept humility and hardship for the sake of the mission—exhibiting the very character he calls them to in this passage.

Paul's focus is on living in unity. It's quite possible verses 4–6 were a common part of worship that he uses here to give the unity idea the full foundation it deserves. Given the struggle often caused by the different ethnic and religious backgrounds (Jewish and "other") of the people who made up this Ephesian community, it's easy to understand the emphasis on unity. You can imagine the kinds of us/them ways of thinking he's trying to help them overcome. He wants them to understand themselves as one people, with one source, and one purpose. Paul knew all too well that division and conflict are some of the quickest ways to derail God's mission.

GATHERING

1. Before this group, what was the last one you joined (team, club, fantasy sport, etc.)?

    What was the best part of being in that group?

FINDING OUR STORIES IN THE STORY

As a prisoner for the Lord, then, I urge you to live a life worthy of the calling you have received. ² Be completely humble and gentle; be patient, bearing with one another in love. ³ Make every effort to keep the unity of the Spirit through the bond of peace.

⁴ There is one body and one Spirit, just as you were called to one hope when you were called; ⁵ one Lord, one faith, one baptism; ⁶ one God and Father of all, who is over all and through all and in all.—**Ephesians 4:1–6 (NIV)**

2. Imagine sitting in the room where this letter was first read. How would you have responded during the Q & A session that followed?

   a. Sounds good, but is that even possible?

   b. Are you kidding me? Gentleness and patience? He's obviously never met me.

   c. That's what I've always longed for.

   d. I've always just found it easier to work by myself.

   e. Other _____ .

3. What do you think Paul means when he says we are to "live a life worthy of our calling"?

4. Why might unity be so important when we're living out our calling?

BECOMING LIKE JESUS

Paul reminds us that God's Spirit (the Holy Spirit) helps us with our steps toward becoming like Jesus.

5. What is the first step you may need to take toward a life of unity and peace, THIS WEEK?

   If people lived in unity, what difference would you expect to see in your community?

OUR MISSION (Living out our potential with an accountable community)

Each time we meet we'll end the session by everyone choosing a new *Mission*—a way to serve—that we will attempt to complete before the next meeting. This is a chance to practice what we've been studying. The *Mission* can be as simple as greeting a neighbor or being courteous to our server at dinner.

Remember, we can be confident that God's Spirit is already at work where we will do our mission, before we arrive.

■ CHOOSING THE MISSION

6. Who in your life, right now, might you struggle to show humility, gentleness, or patience to? (A co-worker, family member, neighbor, etc.)

   To preserve confidence, DON'T write their name. Instead write a "code word" to remind yourself.

   _____

7. How do you plan to live out humility, gentleness, or patience in this relationship this coming week?

   _____

   _____

   [We'll report back to the group at the next meeting, keeping the name anonymous.]

PRAYING TOGETHER

- How can this group pray for you? *(Group leader: Make a list.)*

- *Group Leader: Call out the various concerns from the list. Allow the group to briefly pray silently for each one.*

- *Group Leader: Close with a verbal prayer asking God to guide in the missions this week.*

TO PREPARE FOR NEXT MEETING, EACH GROUP MEMBER
SHOULD COMPLETE
The APEST Personal Vocational Assessment
at
www.5Qcentral.com

BRING YOUR RESULTS PAGES TO THE NEXT MEETING!

SESSION 2: LIVING OUT DIVERSITY

> **NOTE**: If you were unable to complete
> **The APEST Personal Vocational Assessment** at **www.5Qcentral.
> com**, use the definitions in *Getting Started*.
>
> On a scale of 1–5 (1 being the strongest), rate yourself on your
> gifting areas. Later you will want to take the Assessment to see how
> your rating compares.

THE CONTEXT

When we get to verse 7 of Ephesians 4, we see that the talk of unity was not at the expense of our specific, vocational wiring. Unity is the context, but we each have a unique and diverse role to play.

There's some uncertainty about which example of Jesus "ascending" and "descending" Paul is talking about here (whether Jesus descending to earth from heaven, descending to hell after his crucifixion, or his Spirit descending on us after he ascended to heaven). But whichever he's referring to, the fact is that Jesus continually and willingly offered himself to us. AND he's at work way beyond the narrow scope of reality that we see and know and live in. So, Jesus (who lived these gifts out first) offers them to us so we can participate in accomplishing his mission anywhere and everywhere. And it's only when we're all engaged that holistic renewal and restoration is possible.

In *Getting Started* we noted that the biblical gift names may seem strange to us. But all these "roles" or "gifting areas" come from specific types of roles either in Greco-Roman culture and/or from Paul's Jewish background.

For example,
* An **Apostle** was someone who served as an emissary, carrying out a leader's mission under that leader's authority.

- A **Prophet** recalls the Jewish tradition of those who heard from God and spoke God's word to the people—often challenging injustices and the mistreatment of marginalized people.

- An **Evangelist** was a herald; someone who announced good news.

- A Pastor literally means **Shepherd**. (That's why we're using the term.) It recalls images of caring, gathering, providing for, and protecting.

- A **Teacher** is probably the most common term to us because it is a role of instruction and training that we've experienced.

Remember, Jesus gave himself (his gifts) to the church so his mission would continue on earth. And because each person has the image of Jesus planted inside, we as individuals are also wired to live out the APEST gift areas of our vocation—both in a faith community and in those places where we live, work, and play.

As we discussed earlier, we will express some of the APEST areas more strongly than others. Then we'll help one another grow in the weaker areas to become more like Jesus. This means we need each other to express the fullness of Jesus.

A word about *VOCATION.*

When you hear the word VOCATION, think about an umbrella that arches over all the various parts of your life. The goal is to find our over-arching VOCATION, such as "caring for hurting people." Under that umbrella, as much as possible, we want to bring all the pieces of our life together, including whatever we do to earn money.

For example, if I'm mopping floors in a store I can make that work part of my Vocation by paying attention to the needs of other employees or customers who I come in contact with—and serving them. So, I'm not simply cleaning a floor. This change of my focus makes my floor cleaning a piece of my greater Vocation "umbrella."

We can do that with all the parts of our lives where we live, work, and play.

One other thought. Sometimes the term *VOCATIONAL CALL* is used to describe that inner sense that "this is what I was made for." Pay attention to that urging. It may be God's Spirit guiding you.

GATHERING

1. Let's check in from our first MISSION.

   Who did you show humility, patience, or gentleness to?

   What difference (if any) did it make in that relationship?

FINDING OUR STORIES IN THE STORY

⁷ But to each one of us grace has been given as Christ apportioned it.
⁸ This is why it says:
"When he ascended on high, he took many captives and gave gifts to his people."
⁹ (What does "he ascended" mean except that he also descended to the lower, earthly regions? ¹⁰ He who descended is the very one who ascended higher than all the heavens, in order to fill the whole universe.) ¹¹ So Christ himself gave the apostles, the prophets, the evangelists, the pastors and teachers, ¹² to equip his people for works of service, so that the body of Christ may be built up—Ephesians 4:7–12 (NIV)

2. When you think about Jesus offering each of us grace/gifting to be part of his mission, how does that make you feel?

   a. Wow, that sounds like a lot of responsibility.

   b. I guess if it's coming from him, anything could be possible.

   c. How do I figure out what that's supposed to look like in my life?

   d. Other _____ .

23

3. Assuming that Jesus is God, why do you think he decided to gift his followers (the Church) with the resources to accomplish his mission, instead of just doing it himself?

    a. Jesus wasn't sure how to do the missional work on earth while living back in heaven.

    b. Jesus' early followers begged him to let them help.

    c. We are best when we're connected to God's story of transformation.

    d. He wanted us to know how amazing it is to partner in his work.

    e. Other _____ .

4. Looking at your results from *The APEST Personal Vocational Assessment*, which two areas were your highest scores?

    [Remember! The scores are not to be prescriptive for how you should live. But they are a realistic and reliable starting point for you to discover your larger VOCATION—how you're wired for mission/ministry.]

    Were the results what you expected or were you surprised?

    Do they reflect how you identify yourself?

    Why or why not?

5. How might your strongest APEST areas get lived out inside this group or your larger faith community? Give at least one example.

    In YOUR "marketplace" (where you live, work, and play)?

BECOMING LIKE JESUS

6. Pick one of your weaker APEST areas.

   What might be a first, good step toward growing more like Jesus in that area?

   How can this group help you take that first step this week?

OUR MISSION (Living out our potential with an accountable community)

Again this week we'll declare a mission we want to try. And we'll trust God's Spirit to guide us since the Spirit is working there before us.

■ *CHOOSING THE NEXT MISSION*

   How or where can you use your strongest APEST areas to serve someone this week?
   (Make sure it's someone different than who you served last week.)

   Write your goal below.

   _____

   _____

Remember that we'll all report back to the group at the next meeting.

PRAYING TOGETHER

- If possible, form a circle.

- Each person pray a brief, silent prayer for the person on your left. Ask God to bless their mission that's coming this week.

- If there is a volunteer who will pray out loud (if not, the group leader will pray), thank God for the diversity in this group—how God has made each one with special giftings for Jesus' mission.

SESSION 3: LIVING WITH MATURITY

THE CONTEXT

This session brings everything together. We've looked at how Jesus wants us to live in unity, with diverse gifts. Now, Paul presents the purpose behind this plan.

Paul returns to an image he's used other places in his writing—the picture of a body (diverse parts working together for a unified purpose). He layers the imagery ("being built up," "attaining the whole measure," "growing," "becoming mature") to speak of the growth and wholeness that only comes when we live out Jesus' purpose together, in our own specific ways. This is how we, the faith-community we're part of, and the mission become all they were meant to be! The alternative is continuing to live as infants or as a boat tossed on the waves—a prospect that probably would have struck fear into the heart of Paul's listeners.

Paul is also clear that Jesus is the head of this body. This frees us to live out our specific purpose without the need to wield power or emphasize certain types of giftedness over others. The body is his, and through him it grows into its full potential.

GATHERING

1. What insight have you discovered about your strongest APEST gifting area since our last meeting?

    Any new ideas about your *Vocational Call*?

FINDING OUR STORIES IN THE STORY

¹¹ *So Christ himself gave the apostles, the prophets, the evangelists, the pastors and teachers,* ¹² *to equip his people for works of service, so that the body of Christ may be built up* ¹³ *until we all reach unity in the faith and in the knowledge of the Son of God and become mature, attaining to the whole measure of the fullness of Christ.*

¹⁴ *Then we will no longer be infants, tossed back and forth by the waves, and blown here and there by every wind of teaching and by the cunning and craftiness of people in their deceitful scheming.* ¹⁵ *Instead, speaking the truth in love, we will grow to become in every respect the mature body of him who is the head, that is, Christ.* ¹⁶ *From him the whole body, joined and held together by every supporting ligament, grows and builds itself up in love, as each part does its work.*—**Ephesians 4:12–16 (NIV)**

2. If you had been Paul, what image might you have used to help the faith community understand their purpose from verses 14–16?

   If you have a drawing tool, take FIVE minutes to create a picture. If not, just imagine it, so you can explain it to the group.

   When you're done, go around the circle one at a time. Let each person show their picture and explain their "image."

3. What do you think happens to the community and Jesus' mission if there are people not living out their purpose like Paul describes here? If the community is missing certain gifts?

4. If Jesus called you into his office, and offered to answer ANY question about this Bible reading, what would be the first question you'd ask him?

   Why that question?

BECOMING LIKE JESUS

5. What do you think is the biggest road-block to your role of helping/ encouraging others to mature in following Jesus?

6. It may seem easy to use our gift areas to help one another inside the faith community. But how might you live out your specific part of Jesus' mission in your everyday life (where you live, work, or play)?

   a. Yell at people on the street corner.

   b. Give money to someone who is really different than me.

   c. Take a group to the park and talk to strangers to see if we can help them.

   d. Walk around my neighborhood with my dog.

   e. Introduce myself to a neighbor I don't know.

   f. Other _____ .

OUR MISSION (Living out our potential with an accountable community)

■ *REPORT FROM YOUR LAST MISSION*

What do we need to celebrate about your last mission?

What might you do different the next time?

■ *CHOOSING THE NEXT MISSION*

Find a new situation where you can experiment with one of your gifting areas—serving someone without asking anything in return. Where will it be?

_____

_____

PRAYING TOGETHER

- Make a list of concerns to pray for.

- TWO or THREE volunteers pray for the group concerns and upcoming missions.

- *Group Leader: Close with a group blessing (a good word from God).*

SESSION 4: LIFE AS AN APOSTLE

THE CONTEXT

We've looked at Ephesians 4 to get the grand picture that Paul presents of how Jesus has equipped his community—the church—to carry out his mission by giving himself, his gifts, and sending his Spirit.

Now we'll look back into the Gospels to see how Jesus lived out each of the specific gift areas that he gave to the church. We'll take them one at a time over the next five sessions.

This first term, APOSTLE, may have the toughest reputation to overcome. It first describes Jesus—the original Apostle (the "sent one")—who came to earth as a human. Later (and maybe most well known) Apostle was used to refer to those 12 men who knew Jesus in flesh-and-blood; who carried on his mission, purpose, and authority. Since then though, you may have experienced the term being used (rather misused) to identify dictatorial, power-seeking church leaders. So identification as one who has Apostolic gifting may make you frown, roll your eyes, or just confuse you.

So, let's see if we can resurrect the title Apostle with some healthy definitions—and break it out of the limited way it's been used in the past. The *Getting Started* section gave us some initial ideas of how we should understand this gifting area.

The Apostle gifting area includes people who can see the big picture, who network, connect the dots, and take the mission into places it's never gone before. They may be explorers, strategists, church-planters, risk-takers, change-agents...those who lead the way into new and unknown places.

During this session, we'll take a look at these original disciples/apostles who Jesus first trusted his mission to, and how they took his message to new places and audiences. It's interesting that Jesus (as a first-century Jewish rabbi) called normal guys to be his followers, then pretty quickly sent them out to serve with his authority and power. Most rabbis of his day waited for followers to come and request to become disciples—and then only chose the best and brightest. And most likely it would be years before they were trusted to teach in the rabbi's name or step into their own role of authority. But with Jesus, *he* invites, *he* empowers, and *he* sends these every-day people, with only a little training, out into the mission, in the same way he wants to send us.

GATHERING

1. Think back to your elementary school years when teams were chosen for gym class. When were you usually "drafted"?

    a. I was always the very first.
    b. I avoided team play.
    c. I was one of the middle people chosen.
    d. I was the last one, after all the others.

    What did it feel like when you were finally chosen?

FINDING OUR STORIES IN THE STORY

[13] When morning came, he called his disciples to him and chose twelve of them, whom he also designated apostles: [14] Simon (whom he named Peter), his brother Andrew, James, John, Philip, Bartholomew, [15] Matthew, Thomas, James son of Alphaeus, Simon who was called the Zealot, [16] Judas son of James, and Judas Iscariot, who became a traitor.—**Luke 6:13–16 (NIV)**

[9] When Jesus had called the Twelve together, he gave them power and authority to drive out all demons and to cure diseases, [2] and he sent them

out to proclaim the kingdom of God and to heal the sick. ³ He told them: "Take nothing for the journey—no staff, no bag, no bread, no money, no extra shirt. ⁴ Whatever house you enter, stay there until you leave that town. ⁵ If people do not welcome you, leave their town and shake the dust off your feet as a testimony against them." ⁶ So they set out and went from village to village, proclaiming the good news and healing people everywhere.
—Luke 9:1–6 (NIV)

2. In your mind's eye become one of the chosen 12.

   What emotions are you experiencing as Jesus gives directions for the upcoming, on-the-job Apostle-training, when he says, "Don't take anything with you. Instead go find a place to stay in whatever town you end up in. By the way, do some healing and cast out some demons while you're there."

   a. Spitless (tongue sticking to the roof of my mouth).

   b. Confident! (I'm sure to get my face painted into da Vinci's "Last Supper.")

   c. Frightened (but I assume Jesus knows what he's doing).

   d. Unsure (but willing to try).

   e. Other _____ .

3. What might be the significance that Jesus "also designated" them as "apostles" (verse 6:13)?

4. Why is it important that they are more than disciples?

   Why do you think Jesus sent his disciples/apostles out without any of the normal things that make us secure and prepared for a journey?

5. How does this story help to define what an Apostle looks like, acts like, lives like?

BECOMING LIKE JESUS

6. Who do you know that doesn't work for a church but seems to live out the characteristics of an "Apostle"?

   What do they do that makes them seem "Apostle-like"?

7. When you think about growing in the "Apostle" part of your life, the first step should probably be:

OUR MISSION (Living out our potential with an accountable community)

■ *REPORT FROM YOUR LAST MISSION*

How did you serve since the last Village Group meeting?

Where did you recognize God working through you?

■ *CHOOSING THE NEXT MISSION*

As we each choose our next mission, we're going to try serving like Jesus' disciples did, all in Apostolic ways. This will be a good way for all of us to stretch a little, and experiment with something different.

Assuming that APOSTLE is not a strong area for you, you might want to ask questions like, "Where do I need to take a risk that makes me a little uncomfortable?" Or "Where can I do something totally new?" Or "How might I connect people that should work together better than alone?" "Where can I make a connection with someone who would not expect a Christian to be there, like in a community project or environmental service?"

Write an idea of how or where you plan to serve this week.

_____

_____

8. How can this group help you accomplish this week's mission?

    a. Someone please call me!

    b. Pray that I survive!

    c. Text when you can.

    d. Other _____ .

PRAYING TOGETHER

- Group members share celebrations and concerns.

- Make a list of items to pray about.

    Are there specific ways that group members can be the answer to the prayers of other group members?

- Two or three volunteers BRIEFLY pray for the items on the prayer list.

- *Group leader: Close the prayer time.*

SESSION 5: LIFE AS A PROPHET

THE CONTEXT

In this session we look at the role of Prophet. It's important to remember that all the New Testament writers (including Paul) would have drawn their understanding of the "prophetic role" largely from the historical prophets of the Jewish scriptures (what we call the Old Testament).

Depending on your background or experience, you may think of prophetic speaking (or "prophecy") as predicting the future. However, in the Old Testament, the prophet's primary role was to hear what God wanted to say and then speak that message to the community. There were times when this message had future implications, but the message was first directed toward a specific situation. Usually, the prophetic message was to help the people realize how far off they were from God's desire—especially their practices of justice and right-living toward those who were vulnerable, in and around their community.

Prophetic messages were often convicting and carried a note of judgment. As you might expect, these challenging messages were often not well received!

So, when Jesus came on the scene and began to live into this prophetic role, it should be no surprise that he described his mission in terms of Israel's primary prophet, Isaiah. And he centered on care and rescue for those who are vulnerable and marginalized.

The author Luke reports that, just before this session's verses, Jesus had been in the wilderness where Satan challenged his loyalty to God, and his very mission-purpose on earth.

After successfully resisting the tempting shortcuts to his earthly ministry, Jesus headed to his home village—a good place to rest after a difficult time.

In this section of the Bible we find Jesus attending worship in the local synagogue (church) with his family and friends.

The author doesn't tell us, but for some reason the synagogue leader gave Jesus the scripture scrolls to read from.

So, Jesus took this opportunity to step into the Prophet role and declare publicly why he came to earth. And by example, how his followers are to follow.

At first, the people of Jesus' hometown loved what he was saying—Jesus bringing the Lord's favor—as long as it was for them. But in true prophetic fashion, Jesus doesn't leave it there. He pushes them to see God's purpose beyond themselves (in fact even to their enemies… even possibly at their own expense). And in true prophetic fashion, they turn on him and he barely escapes with his life.

GATHERING

1. If you were creating a motto for yourself, at this point in life, what would it be? (10 words or less)

FINDING OUR STORIES IN THE STORY

[14] *Jesus returned to Galilee in the power of the Spirit, and news about him spread through the whole countryside.* [15] *He was teaching in their synagogues, and everyone praised him.*
[16] *He went to Nazareth, where he had been brought up, and on the Sabbath day he went into the synagogue, as was his custom. He stood up to read,* [17] *and the scroll of the prophet Isaiah was handed to him. Unrolling it, he found the place where it is written:*
[18] *"The Spirit of the Lord is on me,*

because he has anointed me
to proclaim good news to the poor.
He has sent me to proclaim freedom for the prisoners
and recovery of sight for the blind,
to set the oppressed free,
¹⁹ *to proclaim the year of the Lord's favor."*
²⁰ *Then he rolled up the scroll, gave it back to the attendant and sat down. The eyes of everyone in the synagogue were fastened on him.* ²¹ *He began by saying to them, "Today this scripture is fulfilled in your hearing."*
²² *All spoke well of him and were amazed at the gracious words that came from his lips. "Isn't this Joseph's son?" they asked.*
²³ *Jesus said to them, "Surely you will quote this proverb to me: 'Physician, heal yourself!' And you will tell me, 'Do here in your hometown what we have heard that you did in Capernaum.'"*
²⁴ *"Truly I tell you," he continued, "no prophet is accepted in his hometown.*
²⁵ *I assure you that there were many widows in Israel in Elijah's time, when the sky was shut for three and a half years and there was a severe famine throughout the land.* ²⁶ *Yet Elijah was not sent to any of them, but to a widow in Zarephath in the region of Sidon.* ²⁷ *And there were many in Israel with leprosy in the time of Elisha the prophet, yet not one of them was cleansed— only Naaman the Syrian."*
²⁸ *All the people in the synagogue were furious when they heard this.* ²⁹ *They got up, drove him out of the town, and took him to the brow of the hill on which the town was built, in order to throw him off the cliff.* ³⁰ *But he walked right through the crowd and went on his way.*—**Luke 4:14–30 (NIV)**

2. You're writing a review of this day-in-the-life-of-Jesus for the *Galilean Times*. What headline will you give the article?

_____

3. Jesus could have chosen any part of the scripture/Bible to read from. Why do you think he picked this section?

4. Why might he have gone on to challenge the people for their lack of belief (in verses 24–27) instead of just leaving them satisfied after verses 18–21?

   a. He liked poking a stick in the "hornet's nest."

   b. He wanted to make the scripture real for them.

   c. The message is incomplete, if it's not all included.

   d. Other _____ .

5. Judging from the crowd's reaction to Jesus' reading and explanation, what do you think it tells us about the Prophet's role?

   a. They don't mind controversy.

   b. They know how to tell the truth, even if it's unpopular.

   c. The *least, lost, last, and alone* people are the priority.

   d. I'm not sure.

   e. Other _____ .

BECOMING LIKE JESUS

6. Describe a time when someone told you something that was really hard to hear but was what you needed to hear.

   How did you react?

   a. I tried to throw them off a cliff.

   b. I said, "Thanks, I needed that."

   c. I grieved because it hurt, but I accepted it because it was true.

   d. Other _____ .

7. Where does Jesus need to help you grow, so you can live more like him in the areas he describes in verses 18–19?

OUR MISSION (Living out our potential with an accountable community)

- ### *REPORT FROM YOUR LAST MISSION*

Where did your serve as an Apostle this week?

How did you see God working?

What did you learn that will help you do differently next time?

- ### *CHOOSING THE NEXT MISSION*

As we choose our missions this coming week, we're going to try serving in Prophetic ways. Again, this will be a good way for all of us to stretch a little, and experiment with something different.

Assuming that PROPHET is not a strong gift area for you, you might be thinking, "I'm not a fortune teller." And that's fine. (In fact, that's not really the goal.)

Some people who have strong prophetic gifting will have insights into what God is saying about how the future can or should look. Others who have the prophetic gifting will be "truth-tellers" of God's message for our current context. And still others will have a passion, like Jesus in this Luke 4 passage, for social justice issues.

Remember—the message will always be for building up—helping others see how to live more completely into God's purpose and mission!

Think words like *principled, correcting, challenging, questioning, passionate, reformer*—for a wide-ranging view of a PROPHET and where you might be able to serve in a prophetic way this week.

How might you challenge, encourage, lead those around you to stretch in how they live out God's justice and compassion in the world?

Write an idea of where you plan to serve.

_____

_____

How can this group help you serve?

PRAYING TOGETHER

* Take a few minutes to discuss items to celebrate since the last meeting and issues you would like the group to pray about.

* Spend time in silence, in your group circle, praying for the person on your right.

* After about a minute, let one volunteer close the prayer time by praying for the group members, and the missions that will be fulfilled by the next meeting.

SESSION 6: LIFE AS AN EVANGELIST

THE CONTEXT

This session we move to the gifting area of EVANGELIST. But before we get to what Paul means when he uses the word, or how Jesus embodies that role, we must at least acknowledge (and probably discard) some of the different preconceptions we may have about an *evangelist* (and related ideas like *evangelical, evangelism*, etc.). The truth is, the way these terms have been used in our contemporary, western context may have nothing to do with what Paul is talking about or how Jesus lived and taught. So we must try seeing in a new way.

First things first.

The word EVANGELIST literally means "one who brings or speaks good news." It's a messenger of "good news."

The idea of "good news" comes from several sources. It was a common term the Roman Empire used to describe the benefits of being ruled by the emperor. His birth or coronation was "good news" for the people because he would bring peace, stability, and prosperity. Unfortunately, if you were a common person (or worse yet, an occupied people like the Jews) those claims of "good news" were mostly empire propaganda.

But the Jewish people had their own notion of "good news" beginning back with the prophet Isaiah (Jesus quoted him in our last session). When the prophets, and in turn Jesus, spoke of "good news" they are talking about something very different from Rome. For Jesus, the Good News is news of a different political reality—the reality of God's peace, love, order, self-sacrifice, and wellbeing—the Kingdom he is sharing, bringing about, inviting us into.

So as we saw last session, as Jesus began his ministry, one of his primary purposes was to declare this "good news to the poor," not good news for the powerful. Jesus' Good News reveals the purposes of God for our world; purposes that challenge, and flip upside-down, the dominating, power-hungry, self-preserving way of the world,

That's Good News!

[As a side note: It's sad that in the current USAmerican culture, when most people think about *evangelism* or *evangelicals*—words that should communicate God's Good News—they tend to think of judgment or "bad news"—of critical, obnoxious people who align themselves with the political Empire.]

In the passage we'll discuss this session, just after Jesus was thrown out of his hometown, He moved on in his region of Galilee to the seaside town of Capernaum—about 20 miles northeast. There he taught, healed and cast out evil spirits.

It's important to keep in mind that this is about as far from the center of Jewish religious and political life as it can be. Yet this is where he spent much of his time, with people who truly needed "good news."

At the end of the Bible section, you'll notice that Jesus again moved on—left the crowds behind because he ... "must proclaim the *Good News of the Kingdom of God*"...to other people in other towns. And Luke tells us Jesus preached (speaking the Good News publicly) in the synagogues (the towns' religious gathering places)—unlike his preferred open-air teaching. Also watch for the many ways Jesus reveals or demonstrates the Good News in this passage.

So let's take a closer look at how Jesus declares Good News and what it might mean for us to share the good, hopeful, and yet empire-challenging news in our own 21st-century context.

GATHERING

1. When was the last time you had to leave a place where you felt really comfortable (e.g., a great party, family reunion, home), but knew it was time to go?

    What would you do differently if you could go back to that time?

    a. Plan my schedule to stay longer.
    b. Make sure to say good-bye to everyone.
    c. Leave sooner.
    d. Other _____ .

FINDING OUR STORIES IN THE STORY

³⁸ *Jesus left the synagogue and went to the home of Simon. Now Simon's mother-in-law was suffering from a high fever, and they asked Jesus to help her.* ³⁹ *So he bent over her and rebuked the fever, and it left her. She got up at once and began to wait on them.*

⁴⁰ *At sunset, the people brought to Jesus all who had various kinds of sickness, and laying his hands on each one, he healed them.* ⁴¹ *Moreover, demons came out of many people, shouting, "You are the Son of God!" But he rebuked them and would not allow them to speak, because they knew he was the Messiah.*

⁴² *At daybreak, Jesus went out to a solitary place. The people were looking for him and when they came to where he was, they tried to keep him from leaving them.* ⁴³ *But he said, "I must proclaim the good news of the kingdom of God to the other towns also, because that is why I was sent."* ⁴⁴ *And he kept on preaching in the synagogues of Judea.*—**Luke 4:38–44 (NIV)**

2. You're a local Jewish broadcaster, milling through the crowd as you watch these healings. How would you describe Jesus' Kingdom—in contrast to the larger Roman Empire or Jewish ruling class?

_____

_____

_____

3. If Jesus' ministry in this town was going so well, and people were still clamoring for him to stay, why do you think he felt the need to leave so quickly?

   a. He was tired of healing and dealing with demons.

   b. The people were just looking for a "healing-show."

   c. His mission was bigger than this little town.

   d. He didn't like the food at Simon's house.

   e. Other _____ .

BECOMING LIKE JESUS

4. If you were thinking about sharing God's Good News in your contemporary context, what messages would you say are primary?

   What avenues/methods/tools might you use?

   _____

   _____

5. As you begin to understand Jesus as an Evangelist, proclaiming "the *Good News* of the Kingdom of God," what might Jesus want to change in how you view the world?

Write one or two thoughts.

_____

_____

OUR MISSION (Living out our potential with an accountable community)

■ REPORT FROM YOUR LAST MISSION

How did you serve as a PROPHET?

Where do you see that God needs to help you grow in your
Prophetic gift area?

What has changed in your understanding of the role of a PROPHET?

■ CHOOSING THE NEXT MISSION

As we choose our next mission, we're going to experiment with serving
as an EVANGELIST. For most people, this will be a stretch into unfamiliar
territory.

Assuming that EVANGELIST is not a strong gift area for you, think about
whom you might take _Good News_ or encouragement to.

Ask yourself:
*   Who might need to know that Jesus loves them?
*   Who do you know that is left out of your favorite group? How might
    you include them?
*   How might you recruit people for a "cause" in your neighborhood that
    needs helpers?
*   Where can your enthusiasm be used to make a difference?

Write an idea of how you plan to serve:

_____

_____

PRAYING TOGETHER

* Take a few minutes to discuss praises since the last meeting. Where have you seen God working?

* What PAST issues do you need to still pray about?

* What NEW concerns does the group need to pray about?

* Let volunteers choose one "issue" to pray for. Then take turns briefly praying for that specific issue.

* *Group leader: Close the meeting with a summary prayer for the group members' missions. After about a minute, let one volunteer close the prayer time by praying for the group members, and the missions that will be fulfilled by the next meeting.*

SESSION 7: LIFE AS A SHEPHERD

THE CONTEXT

Probably the most metaphorical role that Paul describes in Ephesians 4 is the SHEPHERD (where we get the word "pastor" [from Latin]).

As a historically "pastoral" (herding) nation, Israel had experience with shepherds, sheep, and cattle. In fact, many of the forbearers of their faith were shepherds or cattle herders, including Abraham, Rachel, and their greatest king—David, who spent his younger years out in the field with the thankless "youngest-child" job of caring for the sheep.

When looking through the Old Testament, many of the hints toward the coming Messiah refer to a shepherd of God's people.

In Jesus' time, though, shepherding was frowned upon. Shepherds were outcasts of society. They weren't even trusted to be witnesses or to testify in court (which makes it all the more amazing that God chose shepherds to be the very first witnesses of Jesus' birth).

But more than just being despised, shepherds were "unclean" (in a culture who's leaders, called Pharisees, were completely caught up in the necessity of staying "ceremonially clean"). This meant that the religious leaders wouldn't be caught dead near sheep or those that cared for them.

In light of this, Jesus was intentionally controversial when he told stories of lost sheep. It would have made his self-identification as a *Shepherd-leader* in this passage all the more difficult to take (or understand) for those in religious-authority positions. But as we'll see, that may be exactly his point.

Sheep are not the smartest animals, though they are usually obedient. So, it would have been normal for those in authority positions to think of the *common* people in these terms. But Jesus chose not only to identify with them (in spite of the "unclean connotations") but to also gather, care for, lead, and even humbly lay down his life for them.

This was a totally different model of leadership and authority. And you'll notice how Jesus intentionally contrasted these differing leadership models—between his and that of the Pharisees—in this Bible section.

GATHERING

1. CHOOSE ONE:

   What experience have you had with sheep? OR

   What's your favorite childhood nursery rhyme or song about sheep?

2. How would you describe sheep from this experience or rhyme?

   a. They're just dumb animals.

   b. I always thought they were cute.

   c. They're always getting lost.

   d. My childhood was deprived. I have no memory of a nursery rhyme about sheep.

   e. Other _____ .

FINDING OUR STORIES IN THE STORY

[1] "Very truly I tell you Pharisees, anyone who does not enter the sheep pen by the gate, but climbs in by some other way, is a thief and a robber. [2] The one who enters by the gate is the shepherd of the sheep. [3] The gatekeeper opens the gate for him, and the sheep listen to his voice. He calls his own sheep by name and leads them out. [4] When he has brought out all his own, he goes on ahead of them, and his sheep follow him because they know his voice. [5] But

they will never follow a stranger; in fact, they will run away from him because they do not recognize a stranger's voice." ⁶ Jesus used this figure of speech, but the Pharisees did not understand what he was telling them.

⁷ Therefore Jesus said again, "Very truly I tell you, I am the gate for the sheep. ⁸ All who have come before me are thieves and robbers, but the sheep have not listened to them. ⁹ I am the gate; whoever enters through me will be saved. They will come in and go out, and find pasture. ¹⁰ The thief comes only to steal and kill and destroy; I have come that they may have life, and have it to the full.

¹¹ "I am the good shepherd. The good shepherd lays down his life for the sheep. ¹² The hired hand is not the shepherd and does not own the sheep. So when he sees the wolf coming, he abandons the sheep and runs away. Then the wolf attacks the flock and scatters it. ¹³ The man runs away because he is a hired hand and cares nothing for the sheep.

¹⁴ "I am the good shepherd; I know my sheep and my sheep know me— ¹⁵ just as the Father knows me and I know the Father—and I lay down my life for the sheep. ¹⁶ I have other sheep that are not of this sheep pen. I must bring them also. They too will listen to my voice, and there shall be one flock and one shepherd. ¹⁷ The reason my Father loves me is that I lay down my life—only to take it up again. ¹⁸ No one takes it from me, but I lay it down of my own accord. I have authority to lay it down and authority to take it up again. This command I received from my Father."—**John 10:1–18 (NIV)**

3. According to Jesus, what are the Shepherd's primary responsibilities?

    a. Getting water for the sheep.

    b. Catching wolves.

    c. Protecting the sheep.

    d. Chasing down lost sheep.

    e. Other _____ .

4. What's the MOST IMPORTANT point you noticed about the relationship between the sheep and the shepherd?

5. Jesus uses both the "Gate" analogy and the "Shepherd" analogy to describe himself to the Pharisees.

   What do you think the difference is between the *gate* and *shepherd?*

   How might Jesus be both (gate and shepherd)?

BECOMING LIKE JESUS

6. If Jesus called you to meet him at the sheep pen, what do you think he'd want to teach you about caring for sheep (people)?

7. As Jesus-followers, what might living as a SHEPHERD look like to the people in your neighborhood?

   a. Building a fence or stone wall around my neighbors' houses.
   b. Patrolling the neighborhood to make sure no one sneaks out of their houses at night.
   c. Finding ways to gather together and build relationships.
   d. Looking for ways to serve my neighbors.
   e. I'm not really sure.
   f. Other _____ .

OUR MISSION (Living out our potential with an accountable community)

■ *CHOOSING THE NEXT MISSION*

Describe your mission as an EVANGELIST in two or three words.

_____

What was the best part of serving as an EVANGELIST?

What previous ideas about EVANGELISTS have changed in your mind?

■ *CHOOSING THE NEXT MISSION*

As we choose our mission to serve as SHEPHERDS this week, remember that this not a mission just for people who lead ministries, like pastors.

Where might you offer care to someone who needs special attention or protection? (Maybe you're already doing it as a first-responder in your community.)

To help you focus on being a SHEPHERD, think about words like:
 Peace-making
 Defending
 Nurturing
 Protecting
 Reconciling
 Care-giving

WRITE AN IDEA OF HOW YOU PLAN TO SERVE:

_____

_____

PRAYING TOGETHER

- What praise items, since our last session, do you need to share with the group?

- What do you need the group to pray with you about or help you face?

- If you have time, go around the group circle and have each person pray this one-sentence blessing for the person on their RIGHT:

  "Dear God, this is **(your name)**.

  Please bless **(their name)** this week by

  meeting their need for _____ .

  Amen."

- If you're uncomfortable praying out loud, just pray silently to yourself. When you're done say "Amen" (which means, "let it be so") and the next person will know it's their turn to pray.

- When all have prayed, take time to encourage one another as you go out to be a great SHEPHERD.

SESSION 8: LIFE AS A TEACHER

THE CONTEXT

The title or role of TEACHER may be the most familiar way to think of Jesus' and his ministry. And this makes sense given that many of the stories we have of Jesus' life and ministry (the *Gospels*) center around what he said. In these Gospel accounts, the most common way people referred to him was with one of the Greek terms for *teacher* (either *didaskalos*—an instructor of students/disciples, or *grammateus*—an expert in the law and scriptures).

In many ways, Jesus lived into the role of a first-century Jewish "teacher" or "rabbi," which is quite different from what it means to be a teacher today. But even in his own time Jesus' method and message didn't often fit their expectations.

It didn't take long, after Jesus began his ministry, for the crowds to begin growing. Both because of the way he taught and because of the miracles he performed, the word spread quickly, and soon the crowds were large like in this passage.

As mentioned in previous sessions, Jesus usually taught in the outskirts of Israel rather than in the urban center of Jerusalem, and so this diverse crowd was made up of not just a cross-section of Israelites but also people from the Decapolis ("10 Cities" full of non-Jews, on the east side of the Jordan River).

The majority of the crowd seemed to be the social and spiritual outcasts, unlike the religious leaders (those "insiders" often standing around the fringes in judgment). These outcasts would have resonated immediately with Jesus' teaching in this section, starting with the "poor in spirit."

Since Jesus' primary work was growing his disciples (those closest followers) into spiritually mature people who could later be unleashed as leaders of his movement, he kept them close where they received the most explanation of his sometimes-puzzling teachings. The remainder of the crowd gathered around them, to listen in.

On this mountainside, at this time, the people saw no great signs or wonders. Instead they heard Jesus' declaration of his Kingdom purpose and plan. And while they may have previously heard other teachers explain what it meant to be *truly blessed*, Jesus' teaching quickly began to reflect a different way of life; one that stood in sharp contrast to other religious and political leaders.

In fact, at the end of this teaching time, the Bible tells us that the people marveled at his teaching because he spoke as a person with authority, unlike their religious leaders (see Matthew 7:28–29).

GATHERING

1. Describe the largest crowd you were ever in.

    Why were you there?

2. How did you feel?

    a. Lost among so many people.
    b. Really excited to feel the energy of the crowd.
    c. A bit terrorized that I might get crushed.
    d. No special feeling. Just wanted to go home.
    e. Other _____ .

FINDING OUR STORIES IN THE STORY

4:25 Large crowds from Galilee, the Decapolis, Jerusalem, Judea and the region across the Jordan followed him.

5:1 Now when Jesus saw the crowds, he went up on a mountainside and sat down. His disciples came to him, 2 and he began to teach them. He said:

*3 **"Blessed are the poor in spirit,***
  for theirs is the kingdom of heaven.
*4 **Blessed are those who mourn,***
  for they will be comforted.
*5 **Blessed are the meek,***
  for they will inherit the earth.
*6 **Blessed are those who hunger and thirst for righteousness,***
  for they will be filled.
*7 **Blessed are the merciful,***
  for they will be shown mercy.
*8 **Blessed are the pure in heart,***
  for they will see God.
*9 **Blessed are the peacemakers,***
  for they will be called children of God.
*10 **Blessed are those who are persecuted because of righteousness,***
  for theirs is the kingdom of heaven.

11 "Blessed are you when people insult you, persecute you and falsely say all kinds of evil against you because of me. 12 Rejoice and be glad, because great is your reward in heaven, for in the same way they persecuted the prophets who were before you.—**Matthew 4:25–5:12 (NIV)**

3. Close your eyes and imagine settling into the grass on this hillside. Smell the air. Then carefully watch the crowd around you.

What do you notice first?

a. The scowling religious leaders.

b. The strange people, not like you.

c. The amazed crowd, sitting so quietly.

d. Some people snickering at Jesus' crazy ideas.

e. The way Jesus's teaching both captivates and confuses the audience.

f. Other _____ .

4. What, ONE or TWO of Jesus' statements seem the most counter-cultural or against normal expectations?

_____

_____

BECOMING LIKE JESUS

5. Does anything Jesus said give you hope for your future?

If so, what is it?

If not, why not?

6. If you were one of the disciples sitting beside Jesus, what would you want to ask him when he was done teaching?

7. How might Jesus need to help you live more like what he's teaching here? Write down one idea.

_____

_____

8. Where do you need this group to help you take that next step in following Jesus this week?

OUR MISSION (Living out our potential with an accountable community)

■ **REPORT FROM YOUR LAST MISSION**

What did you do for your Shepherding mission?

Where did you do it?

Do you think the SHEPHERD role is one of your strongest passions?

Why or why not?

■ **CHOOSING THE NEXT MISSION**

This week we'll experiment with serving on our mission as a TEACHER. Since we are quite familiar with teachers, we may need to EXPAND our thinking a little before starting.

Think of ways you might serve as one who:
   ... Speaks of and promotes a different, more compassionate way of life in your work, home, or other context
   ... Guides someone who needs wisdom or insight in making a difficult decision.
   ... Shows children how to make a new and fun discovery.
   ... Helps coach someone to learn a new skill.
   ... Guides discussion toward a healthy solution in a complex work situation.

From those brainstorming thoughts, how do you plan to serve *specifically*?

_____

_____

_____

_____

PRAYING TOGETHER

- Review the prayer requests that were shared last meeting.

- What answers do you need to give praise for?
  What issues need continued prayer?

- How can the group members pray for one another this week?

- Let several group members volunteer to pray a one-sentence prayer for each of the prayer concerns.

- *Group Leader: Give a blessing as the group dismisses, to go to their lives on mission.*

Before you dismiss this session, plan to have a
Celebration Party as part of your ninth gathering.

At your ninth session you'll celebrate the weeks you've had together
in this missional study; AND you'll decide where to go from here,
as group members and as a Village Group.

SESSION 9: LIVING INTO THE FUTURE— A CELEBRATION

THE CONTEXT

Jesus would feel right at home at a Celebration Party. You may remember that his first miracle was creating the best wine at a wedding. And his critics often tried to shame him by calling him a glutton or drunkard because he made a habit of hanging out at parties with the "wrong kind of people."

We finish these sessions, back where we began.

We've covered a lot of territory since Session 1 as we've experimented with missional living, working both in our strongest ministry callings/giftings and those where we need to keep growing. We've discovered that each Jesus-follower is called to a vocation of ministry—whether teaching in an elementary school, carrying on a conversation at the office water cooler, hanging out at the neighborhood playground, or pastoring in a local church. Wherever we live, work, and play is where God wants to use us in mission. And God's Spirit (the Holy Spirit) has equipped us with giftings/passions for effectiveness in our particular ministry setting.

However, it's important to remember that discovering both our strongest and less-developed ministry giftings on an APEST Assessment tool is only part of discovering our missional place in God's Kingdom work. We also need to look at our
- *life experiences,*
- *personality type* (such as introvert or extrovert),
- *the seasons of life God has grown us in,* and
- *how we view our ministry identity.*

In addition, as we're learning, all those pieces must be considered within a group of Jesus-followers; a Village where we help one another grow more into the image of Jesus for the sake of others.

Thus, our vocation is a journey of adventure that flexes and grows as we become more spiritually mature.

In this session, we'll review what we've seen over the previous weeks and look toward the next chapter of this group's life.

The group has several choices:

- The group could simply stop meeting, but that's not the best choice since we all need to be connected to a Village Group.
- One option is to take a break for a while, then come back together (make sure to set the return date today).
- Another option is to stop meeting as THIS specific group of people and re-form, with other people, into other groups (upset the "fruit basket"). This can be a really healthy process because we sometimes feel stuck in a group.
- A third option is to move forward with this group and start into a new set of studies.

One great resource is *Radical Journey*, a study of Jesus' Sermon on the Mount. In *Radical Journey*, the text is broken into 20 chunks, with each week including a small portion of the Sermon on the Mount, individual study, Village Group time, then a Mission opportunity (similar to what you've each been doing the last eight sessions).

So as you celebrate the last eight sessions with food and drink, take time for:

- **personal reflection.**
- **Then make a decision about your future as a group.**

GATHERING

1. If this group never met again, what part of the time in this group would you most miss?

FINDING OUR STORIES IN THE STORY

¹ As a prisoner for the Lord, then, I urge you to live a life worthy of the calling you have received. ² Be completely humble and gentle; be patient, bearing with one another in love. ³ Make every effort to keep the unity of the Spirit through the bond of peace. ⁴ There is one body and one Spirit, just as you were called to one hope when you were called; ⁵ one Lord, one faith, one baptism; ⁶ one God and Father of all, who is over all and through all and in all. ⁷ But to each one of us grace has been given as Christ apportioned it. ⁸ This is why it says:

"When he ascended on high,
he took many captives
and gave gifts to his people."

⁹ (What does "he ascended" mean except that he also descended to the lower, earthly regions? ¹⁰ He who descended is the very one who ascended higher than all the heavens, in order to fill the whole universe.) ¹¹ So Christ himself gave the apostles, the prophets, the evangelists, the pastors and teachers, ¹² to equip his people for works of service, so that the body of Christ may be built up ¹³ until we all reach unity in the faith and in the knowledge of the Son of God and become mature, attaining to the whole measure of the fullness of Christ.

¹⁴ Then we will no longer be infants, tossed back and forth by the waves, and blown here and there by every wind of teaching and by the cunning and craftiness of people in their deceitful scheming. ¹⁵ Instead, speaking the truth in love, we will grow to become in every respect the mature body of him who is the head, that is, Christ. ¹⁶ From him the whole body, joined and held together by every supporting ligament, grows and builds itself up in love, as each part does its work.—**Ephesians 4:1–16 (NIV)**

PERSONAL REFLECTION

2. What was the most difficult mission you tried during these weeks?

   What made it difficult?

   a. I didn't like the people I was serving.
   b. I never felt like I was serving in one of my strong gifting areas.
   c. I was too busy to focus on the mission.
   d. I'm a rebel. I don't like doing projects when they're assigned.
   e. Other _____ .

3. Using what you've learned from this passage and the time in this group, write a ONE-sentence statement to define how you see your VOCATION today.

   (Remember that we started defining VOCATION back in Session 2 as an umbrella over the various parts of your life. It's usually BIGGER than just what you get paid to do for "work," but should include it.)

   Make the statement specific but open enough to take different shapes as you live into it—like:

   "My vocation is to speak the truth into hard or complex situations," OR

   "My vocation is to care for people who are the least, the lost, the last, the alone."

   _____

   _____

4. How do you need God's Spirit to help you live into your future vocational mission plan?

THE VILLAGE GROUP'S NEXT STEPS IN MISSION

5. How can this group continue to live out it's call to mission—it's APEST?

    a. Keep this group together and meet regularly to keep working on it.

        (Decide on a specific time—at least twice each month, like the FIRST and THIRD Mondays. If you say something vague like "every other week" people will become confused when an extra week comes along in a month.)

        When is your next *check-in* point to re-evaluate your continued group life? Three months? Six months?

    b. Let some members, who think it's time for them to go, move on to something else.

        (Release them without guilt, commission them on to their next mission—grateful that your lives have crossed during this time.)

    c. Assuming that some of the group members want to remain in the group, recruit new members and continue to meet.

        (What will you use for the *relational Bible study* to help you continue encouraging one another to become more like Jesus for the sake of others?)

    d. What other options should the group consider?

        (All ideas are allowed into the discussion.)

Try to make a decision about the Village Group's future before this session dismisses, so everyone can be going the same direction for the future.

What specific decision have you made?

_____

_____

PRAYING TOGETHER

Take time, as the final act of this party, to AFFIRM and COMMISSION one another.

* If you have more than FIVE group members, break into sub-groups of three or four.

* Send each group to a location where they will have some privacy.

* Each person in the sub-group will take a turn on the "Hot-seat." That means they are the center of attention, but may not speak.

* Go around the sub-group, letting each person giving a BRIEF **word of affirmation** about the person on the "Hot-seat." How did you see them living out/serving from their gift areas in mission?

* After each person has given an affirmation, ask one person in the sub-group to pray a **one-sentence prayer of commissioning** for the "Hot-seat" person's future vocational ministry.

* Continue on until everyone has been AFFIRMED and COMMISSIONED.

Once everyone has been affirmed and commissioned, the entire group joins in a huddle, if possible.

Group Leader: Close by praying this traditional blessing over the group:

"God bless you and keep you,
God smile on you and gift you,
God look you full in the face and
Make you prosper."
In the name of the Father, the Son,
And the Holy Spirit. Amen"
(from Numbers 6:24–26, MSG)

GOING FURTHER INTO MATURITY

Check out these great resources for both group and individual growth.

- *Radical Journey*—a 20-week encounter with Jesus in the Sermon on the Mount (Matthew 5–7).

  » Available in a single unit at **www.Lulu.com**.

  » A two-book version is planned for **www.5Qcentral.com**. Check for availability.

- Five great **APEST modules (AQ, PQ, EQ, SQ, TQ)** for a deep-dive study into each gifting area. Available at **www.5Qcentral.com**.

- For information about personal and group coaching/training, contact **Daryl L. Smith** at **DarylSmith432@gmail.com**.

LEADER'S GUIDE:
LEADING A VILLAGE (small) GROUP

FIRST THINGS FIRST...

These notes are primarily for Village Group leaders. However, whether an administrative board, a sports-bar Bible study or something in between, every group should become a community of people who live in love with one another and on mission to those outside the group. So the following guidelines are adaptable to most any setting.

The idea of creating and facilitating a Village Group may be new and scary. You may have been pushed into this role by someone who hands you a paycheck. Someone may have challenged you to a stretching experiment. Or you may have been wondering how to grow your ministry to a deeper level. If any of those scenarios are true, just hang on and watch what happens in the weeks ahead!

SETTING THE STAGE...

The Village Group is a small group of people, exploring the life of Jesus and how to live passionately like him, on his Kingdom mission.

The sessions are NOT just a place to lecture about the Bible; nor a place to give advice (except in rare situations). As the facilitator, you will guide the small group of people on a journey to discover more about who Jesus is and how they are to become more like him.

The PRIMARY PURPOSE of the Village Group is to help the group members—

   ... create healthy relationships (with God and one another),

   ... discover Jesus' Kingdom plan through relational Bible study— connecting the 3 stories (see below),

... become equipped for vocational, missional living, and

... launch into group and personal mission wherever they live, work, and play.

> *If you're an old pro at this VILLAGE GROUP stuff, we trust that this guide will provide a resource to move your group into a more joyful and transparent community—to become a group of people who care deeply for one another and serve from that community.*

A QUICK CHECKLIST...

As the Village Group leader you will guide the group session (topic, time usage, etc.).

• Set the start time and place for the group meetings.

• During the group session, keep the group on track, within the time limits. Usually a group session should last about **1.5 hours**.

• Each session must START and STOP on time. If some want to continue with discussion after the scheduled conclusion time, dismiss everyone and let those who want to stay, stay.

You will not always be able to cover every question or complete every activity. When you must cut off discussion, it is important to give time signals (at least at the 5 minute and 2 minute points before stopping).

People will be energized for the next group session if they haven't felt trapped. You may hear some groans when time is cut short. Explain what you're doing—keeping your word to end the session on time. The complaining means that discussion was going well.

- Make sure that each person has a book or printout of the week's session. Ask people NOT to bring other biblical commentaries, books, etc., to the group, so everyone can stay focused on the specific Bible passage and questions.

  Commentaries shut down conversation as they become the "official correct answer" to any questions.

- Respect each person and their opinions. As you model respect, people will see that differing opinions don't call for rudeness or demeaning behavior.

- Care for group members and their families between meetings—but not alone. Encourage and coordinate (or have someone coordinate) the group members in their care for one another.

- Go FIRST in answering questions early in the group life, unless others respond quickly. It helps to break the ice when you give an example of how you would answer. However, silence for thinking helps the introverts become equal contributors with the extroverts.

- Carefully note that each part of the group session has a specific purpose. Depending on time, you may need to skip some questions; but be sure to include at least one question from each section. And ALWAYS include the *OUR MISSION* and *PRAYING TOGETHER sections*—even if you have to abbreviate or change them slightly. They are vital to everything that the group is about.

- Additional details and descriptions are given below for each section of the Village Group session.

NOW SOME GROUP THEORY...

■ SUBDIVIDE

When a group grows larger than SEVEN people, you need to subdivide the group for at least part of your Village Group session. You may notice that in a group larger than seven, about half of the group members join in discussion while the other half observes.

• The **ENTIRE GROUP** should meet together for the *GATHERING* question(s), a drink, and some food.

• **FOURSOMES** are the best grouping for the *FINDING OUR STORIES IN THE STORY* Bible study and discussion.

  If you can avoid **threesomes**, do it! Threesomes become tiring since each person must maintain intense focus. Foursomes help people relax and introverts will participate.

  You may want to keep **foursomes** for the *BECOMING LIKE JESUS* and *OUR MISSION* sections.

  All group members should join together in one location for *PRAYING TOGETHER* time. Group members can bring concerns they've shared in the foursomes to this time.

• **EIGHTSOMES** or more are great for worship or singing, if you add those elements to the group time.

• While it's important to always plan to birth a new group, subdividing allows a group to grow to almost any size. This is particularly important if a group grows quickly, before an *Apprentice-leader* is ready to take the group leadership. (See *Birth New Groups—Never Split.*)

■ THE VILLAGE GROUP

A *Village Group* goes well beyond the typical small group. It's a place where:
...Everyone belongs,
...People feel safe to tell their story,
...Everyone is being equipped for ministry and service,
...Everyone is cared for,
...There is a common mission, AND
...You can always come home.

• **EVERYTHING BEGINS WITH STORY.** We live stories, we watch stories, we tell stories.

When we learn through story, rather than just memorizing facts, our entire brains and bodies come alive; we naturally remember and apply the learning to future situations in our lives.

This group is designed around THREE STORIES:

▶ The FIRST story is God's story (told through the Bible) that shows God's creative plan for us as amazing humans, our walking away from God's plan, and God's becoming human (Jesus) to call us back home.

▶ The SECOND story is another person's life story, with all its stuff.

▶ The THIRD story is *my* story, with all of its stuff.

Remember, Jesus said that when two or three people gather in his name that he shows up (see Matthew 18:20). So, we can count on that. When the three stories come together in a small group of Jesus followers, amazing things happen.

Every time we meet, we each tell part of our stories in the context of God's story. When the THREE STORIES connect, we discover what it means to be a disciple of Jesus—living in a vital, growing, missional community.

This is called *Relational Bible Study*.

- **RELATIONSHIPS**—We are created for **relationship**. If we are to learn about relating to God or another people, we must wrestle with those relational concepts (like *patience* or *love*) in a small group setting—practicing with people who are different from us.

- **PREFERENCES**—We each have our own learning preferences. Some of us start learning by wanting to know **WHY** what we're studying is important. Others of us just want to know the content—**WHAT**. Still others of us are primarily concerned with **HOW** we can use what we're learning. Then, some of us dream about **WHAT ELSE** we could do with what we learn.

- **INNER CHILD**—All of us have a child inside who wants to be released. These studies will help us "come to Jesus as a little child" (see Matthew 19:14). So prepare to laugh and cry!

- **INDUCTIVE STUDY**—The academic term for what we're doing is INDUCTIVE Bible study. (Letting the text tell us what it means rather than using it to prove or reinforce our ideas.) Inductive study gives people the opportunity to walk into the scripture and dance around in the context—viewing the scene from all angles. Thus, we learn from one another and the Holy Spirit—as we apply the Bible to our everyday lives.

■ **THE QUESTIONS**

Questions are strategically worded and placed where they are to help the three stories connect around the Bible passage.

As the leader of the group, you should know your group. And since you know the *purpose* of the various questions, feel free to rewrite or adapt them for your needs.

In addition, if discussion goes long on particular questions, don't panic, just cut somewhere else. HOWEVER, as you adapt, make sure to pick and choose from each type of question, keeping them in the correct sequence.

■ THE SESSION

• GATHERING

The **GATHERING** question(s) is to get the group thinking about the biblical topic in a non-threatening way; often producing laughter, bringing out positive endorphins and reducing barriers to the deeper questions that are coming.

You may want to "toss" this question into conversation around a coffee pot in the kitchen, before sending FOURSOMES off to various locations to study the Bible passage.

Most of us worry about what to do with our hands if we're standing in a group, so try to get something into each person's hand. They will talk more openly if their hands are occupied, holding a mug or glass.

• FINDING OUR STORIES IN THE STORY

The first two or three questions right after the Bible reading help people put themselves into the scripture passage. This is where *INDUCTIVE* Bible study starts.

The next few questions are to help the group **dig out some of the content**. You may want to add extra questions here, but **do it carefully** so you don't bog the group down or lose sight of the overall purpose. The temptation is to "go deeper" in study, which usually means learning facts instead of building healthy relationships around the Bible section.

• BECOMING LIKE JESUS

This part of the session presents questions that encourage a response to the scripture. Each individual will attempt to apply to their individual lives, what they are discovering from the Bible passage.

Some responses may appear superficial; others really profound and life transforming. As a leader, you must carefully respond to all answers, providing dignity and respect to each group member as they attempt to become transparent.

If you must skip questions due to limited time, always include **at least one question** from this section. Since you know your group, you will decide which one is most important.

During this time, you also have the opportunity to guide the group in *SHEPHERDING* one another. As each person shares where they are being challenged in their growth, the other members can commit to onoourage and support, as each person stretches for their next step in becoming more like Jesus.

- **OUR MISSION**

Each session includes an assignment for group members to serve on *MISSION* before the next Village Group meeting.

Never neglect this section of the Village Group meeting. Living on mission is primary, if we are to grow into the image of Jesus *for the sake of others.* So you may need to re-shape the group session, making sure this section is always included. After a couple of group meetings you'll sense a pattern for your group's time use.

The specific assignment is included in the Village Group session materials.

In addition to the *upcoming MISSION* assignment, there is always time to report from the *previous mission.* If you need to cut the reports shorter due to limited time, consider having people report their *previous missions* in the FOURSOMES, during their *FINDING OUR STORIES IN THE STORY* time.

These assigned, and reported-back, *MISSION* assignments help build a personal ministry pattern into each group member's daily life.

Once a month or so, you will want to find a way to serve together as a group, in your community, your city, or the world. Particularly look for opportunities to partner with agencies or groups who are making a positive difference in your area—whether faith-based or not.

In addition, every group should have an "empty chair." Then each group member remains constantly alert for friends and neighbors to fill the empty chair—to join your Village Group.

It is important to plant the idea of MISSION or SERVICE at the very first gathering of the group; reinforcing it each time the group meets.

- **PRAYING TOGETHER**

As part of each session, you will guide the group in various patterns of prayer so they can join in carrying one another's needs.

Specific prayer guidelines are included in each *PRAYING TOGETHER* part of the Village Group session. Feel free to make adjustments as you sense they are needed. However, try to use a variety of styles like those suggested in the session materials.

Additionally, guidelines listed in the *A WORD ABOUT PRAYING TOGETHER* (below) provide tools to help you introduce prayer to the group, and help each person begin praying aloud.

A Few CAUTIONS:
1. NEVER let anyone "confess another person's sins." People are only allowed to talk about their own issues. You might need to interrupt an overly transparent person. This often happens between couples.
2. Gossip can kill a group. Watch for prayer requests/concerns that are actually cloaked gossip.
3. Sometimes one person may dominate conversation with their struggles for several meetings. As a leader, you may need to talk directly to such a person, in private. A group cannot do therapy for an individual. That takes special care from a professional.

WHO'S READING THE BIBLE...

It's not unusual for people to be called on to read in a group. However, it can strike terror in any introvert or person with reading difficulties. Use these guidelines when preparing to read the Bible passages together as a group—even if you've subdivided into FOURS for the Bible study time.

- Unless you know a person really well, and their reading ability, never surprise a person by calling on them to read. This is especially true when reading the Bible, which may have difficult-to-pronounce words or complicated language structures.

- The best way to prepare a person to read is to ask them before the session starts. Give them the opportunity to review the passage and plan for any difficult words or phrases.

- If a person volunteers to read but then has difficulty getting through a passage, feel free to assist them by giving them a word or two and letting them attempt to continue.

- Thank and compliment readers, particularly when the passage or pronunciations have been difficult.

A WORD ABOUT PRAYING TOGETHER

From session to session you are directed to change the way the group prays. Sometimes you'll want the group all together. Other weeks staying in the FOURS will be best.

If you want your group members to go spitless, just ask them to pray out loud. But if you want to teach them to actually pray for one another, suggest various forms of prayer, in a progressive way.

Here are four levels of prayer that will help get your group started. You will decide when your group members are ready to move from one level to the next. (Think several weeks, not one week to the next.)

Level 1: After the group has shared concerns, *you* pray out loud. As you model praying for the group, forget the special words or phrases you might have heard. That's what scares people out of feeling competent to pray. Just be yourself conversationally with God.

Level 2: After requests have been shared, ask for an equal number of *volunteers* to pray for those requests—each one praying a brief prayer for each request.

Level 3: Invite **two or three** group members to pray, then you conclude. This takes *courage* for those who've never prayed out loud before because you've not assigned them a topic to pray about.

Don't be afraid of silence for a moment or two. If no one prays after a lengthy time of silence, go ahead and pray yourself.

Level 4: Ask the group to sit or stand in a circle and pray out loud around the circle by saying something like, "Dear God, this is ＿＿＿＿＿＿＿ . Thank you for ＿＿＿＿＿＿＿. Amen."

If anyone is too uncomfortable with this, they can pray silently when their turn comes. They will simply say "Amen" to let the next person know when they have completed their silent prayer.

You may also try variations of any of these Levels of Prayer, such as having the group pray silently around the circle for the person on their left.

Before long you'll have the whole group easily praying for one another. They just have to discover that it's safe to say what they're really thinking and feeling without the pressure to produce some form of "magic" words for God.

■ BIRTH NEW GROUPS—NEVER SPLIT

You may not plan to birth a new group during the first few months of your Village Group's life. However, if you continue meeting longer than about 12 months, you'll want to start the birthing process.

Here are a few important tips when introducing the birthing idea to the group members, and when you actually begin birthing a new Village Group.

Always us the term *birthing*. We **never** *split* groups. Birthing is the healthy beginning of another group out of an original Village Group.

Once a group reaches 10 to 12 people, the group needs to start planning the birth. However, "birthing" should be discussed at the very first group meeting, and every meeting thereafter, so no one is surprised.

Remember that you can effectively use **Subdividing** until you're ready for the birth.

Every group must have an *Apprentice* as well as a Leader. When birthing a new group, the **original Leader**, with **three to six** people from the original group, are commissioned to leave the original Village Group to start the new one.

The **Apprentice** stays as leader of the original group. Both groups must then quickly find new Apprentice leaders.

The best way to birth a new group is for the current Leader to collect an affinity group *from the original group* (for example, parents of 2-year-olds). Those three to six people will invite others to join them. They might even start the new group studying something about parenting toddlers. After such an "affinity study" they will move back to their regular Village Group Bible study.

Birthing is enhanced when the original group and the newly-birthed group create a celebration party for the launch. You also might consider periodic *family-reunion parties* for a couple of months.

Everyone is responsible for recruiting new group members to fill the vacancies created by the birth—and to grow the new-birthed group. Never forget the **empty chair**.

■ LAST BUT NOT LEAST

To be most effective in your ministry as a Group Leader, you need to start seeing yourself as a **SHEPHERD** to your Village Group. That's right, a SHEPEHERD, even if that is not your strongest APEST gift area.

Try saying that out loud to yourself:

"I am a Shepherd to this Village Group."

Congratulations, you did it!

One of your primary roles is guiding the group and caring for the group members' needs.

Before you reject the idea outright, think about it for a minute. Your faith community probably has other persons whom you call Shepherd or Pastor. She or he oversees the larger ministry of the congregation. However, you probably noticed that there is no way for one person to meet a congregation's many needs. The best care comes when a small group, led by its Leader, takes responsibility for its team members. You are the *front-line shepherd* to your "*congregation*."

This also gives you the opportunity to recruit those in your group who have the Shepherd gifting/passion, and coach them to begin caring for the other group members.

In other words, you are modeling the life of a disciple. **And disciples disciple others to follow Jesus!**

This Shepherding model may primarily mean leading the Village Group sessions. But it will also include staying alert to the individual emotional, physical, and spiritual needs of your group members. It could also mean hospital visitation or rallying the group for special support of a group member who is facing a crisis.

Here's another way to think of it: **You are a COACH!**

When you read that word *Coach*, your mind may think of coaches you've seen pace the sidelines of a court or field; some yelling, screaming and throwing things—others calmly watching and guiding the team.

Hundreds of years ago, before the word *coach* became a person, it described a vehicle. And that vehicle carried royalty—PRECIOUS CARGO.

Finally, consider a third picture of leading a village group: **You are a MIDWIFE.**

Let that idea soak into your whole being for a moment.

Your role is to help birth new life into individual group members while at the same time guiding the Village Group toward birthing new groups. We should never let our groups become stale, stagnant, or stay the same way forever. That kills community.

So, when you are **Shepherding/Coaching/Midwifing** your Village Group, you are **carrying *precious cargo***. You are helping God's Spirit (the Holy Spirit) move people from where they are right now to where God wants them to be, down the road.

But don't let that overwhelm you.

This is God's ministry, and you have the privilege of partnering with the Holy Spirit, who has been at work long before you got to this place. And you're coaching a group of people who can learn to care for one another.

So have fun watching what you and God can do together to grow your Village Group into an amazing MISSIONAL COMMUNITY!

■ FURTHER RESOURCES

- Check out the many options for coaching and training at **www.5Qcentral.com**.

- Coaching for creating vibrant Village Group ministries or implementing 5Q. Available from the author. Contact Daryl L. Smith (Village Group Trainer, 5Q Coach/Trainer) at **DarylSmith432@gmail.com** or **www.5Qcentral.com**.

CPSIA information can be obtained
at www.ICGtesting.com
Printed in the USA
FSHW012323080619
58728FS